The Gardener and the Orange

AUSTIN RUMPEL
Illustrated by Savannah Lafreniere

For all those who have felt that they might not be enough.

Thank you to our parents,
who have in every way been so incredibly supportive of us.

The Gardener and the Orange
Copyright © 2021 by Austin Rumpel

Published by Lucid Books in Houston, TX
www.LucidBooksPublishing.com

Illustrated by Savannah Lafreniere

All rights reserved. No part of this publication may be reproduced, stored in a retrieval system, or transmitted in any form by any means, electronic, mechanical, photocopy, recording, or otherwise, without the prior permission of the publisher, except as provided for by USA copyright law.

ISBN: 978-1-63296-455-7 Paperback
ISBN: 978-1-63296-456-4 Hardcover
ISBN: 978-1-63296-457-1 eBook

Special Sales: Most Lucid Books titles are available in special quantity discounts. Custom imprinting or excerpting can also be done to fit special needs. For standard bulk orders, go to www.lucidbooksbulk.com. For specialty press or large orders, contact Lucid Books at books@lucidbookspublishing.com.

Take a moment to imagine this:
you are a wonderful little orange
sitting on a tree in an orchard.

On one day in particular, one of the many visitors who come through the orchard stands by your tree, inspects you, and then walks on.

She suddenly stops to look across the dirt pathway and points, saying, "Would you look over there at that tree? Look at those apples! Wow! That is a good-looking fruit tree."

Then the woman lowers her hand and continues walking down the path.

As she walks off, you hang there, a perfectly good and wonderful orange.

Yet now you wonder why you aren't a little bit more like those apples across the path.

You squirm, you wiggle, and you strain.

You clench your teeth and stare intently at those bright red apples.

You think very hard and pray even harder.

Even though you feel slightly better after praying, nothing happens.

Then one day, the Gardener comes by your tree. He looks at each tree as he walks by, inspecting it from top to bottom.

He inspects the tree you hang on
and starts to move on to the next but then stops.
He turns back to your tree and looks directly at you.

"Well hello there, little orange," he says.

"Now hold on a minute." He looks at you,
then across the way at the apple tree.

You blush but decide to quickly answer because, well, this is THE Gardener.

"Uh, yes . . . I am," you say.

"I see how wonderful they are. How bright they are. I even heard a person say that those apples are what fruits should look like."

The Gardener pauses, looks at you, and smiles.

While smiling, the Gardener says, "My dear orange, you are exactly the way you should be."

"I charge you this instant to stop trying to be like an apple! Relax, and be the orange I planted you to be."

The Gardener and the orange said much more to each other that day.

But from that day forward, the orange was able to relax and be free from the pressure of trying to be like an apple.

She continued to grow brighter and more and more colorful.

She did not have to strive to be connected—she already was.

This happened naturally and without her trying extra hard, simply because she was connected to the branch.

She did not have to rush her growth because the Gardener had planted her in his time and took care of the garden himself.

From then on, she simply sat there, abiding in the branch and being the orange the Gardener had planted her to be.

Austin loves to write! He has found that some of the most valuable and wonderful life lessons can be learned through studying nature, story, and the simple rhythms of living. He has worked as a camp counselor, a little league coach, and a youth pastor; he has a BA in Christian ministry from The King's University. He currently lives in Houston, Texas, with his beautiful wife, Anna.

CPSIA information can be obtained
at www.ICGtesting.com
Printed in the USA
LVHW070836240621
690733LV00033B/350